# THE
# LITTLE GIANT® BOOK OF
# GIGGLES

## CHARLES KELLER

*Illustrated by* **JEFF SINCLAIR,**
**DAVE WINTER,**
*and* **DAVE GARBOT**

**STERLING PUBLISHING CO., INC.**
New York

Published by Sterling Publishing Company, Inc.
387 Park Avenue South, New York, N.Y. 10016
This book has been excerpted from
*Awesome Jokes* © 1996 by Charles Keller
*Best Joke Book Ever* text © 1998 by Charles Keller,
illustrations © 1998 by Jeff Sinclair
*Best Knock-Knock Book Ever* © 2000 by Charles Keller
*Best Riddle Book Ever* © 1997 by Charles Keller
*Goofy Jokes & Giggles* © 2001 by Charles Keller
*Kids' Funniest Knock-Knocks* © 2000 by Charles Keller
*Kids' Funniest Riddles* © 2000 by Charles Keller
*Super Silly Riddles* © 2001 by Charles Keller

Distributed in Canada by Sterling Publishing
$^c/_o$ Canadian Manda Group, One Atlantic Avenue, Suite 105
Toronto, Ontario, Canada M6K 3E7
Distributed in Great Britain and Europe by Chris Lloyd
at Orca Book Services, Stanley House, Fleets Lane,
Poole BH15 3AJ, England
Distributed in Australia by Capricorn Link (Australia) Pty. Ltd.
P.O. Box 704, Windsor, NSW 2756 Australia

Sterling ISBN 1-4027-0287-6

# Contents

# 1. Worm-Ups

What kind of hat do birds wear?
*A Robin Hood.*

How do birds get ready to exercise?
*They do worm-ups.*

What is the best way to get rid of a
100-pound worm in your garden?
*Get a 1,000-pound robin.*

What can you do to help a sick bird?
*Get it tweeted.*

Why was Tweety Bird the first one to go to
the hair stylist?
*Because the early bird gets the perm.*

Why did the bird wear a toupee?
*It was a bald eagle.*

What bird goes to church?

*A bird of pray.*

What do you call a frightened woodpecker?

*Chicken of the trees.*

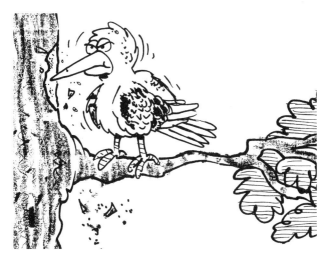

Knock-Knock.
    Who's there?
Owl.
    Owl who?
Owl goes whoo – you got that right.

What kind of bird hunt is never successful?

*A wild goose chase.*

What makes a goose different from other animals?

*Most animals grow up, but a goose grows down.*

Why do people get goose bumps?

*Because camel bumps are too big.*

Knock-Knock.

Who's there?

Goosie.

Goosie who?

Goosie who's at the door.

What do little birds eat at snacktime?
*Chocolate chirp cookies.*

Why do birds fly south for the winter?
*It beats waiting for the bus.*

What happens when you annoy a black bird?
*It goes stark raven mad.*

What do you call a bird in winter?
*A brrrd.*

A woman walked into a pet shop that was having a sale. "Do you have any birds left?" she asked.

"You're in luck," the owner told her. "All that twitters is not sold."

Knock-Knock.

Who's there?

Fiddle.

Fiddle who?

Fiddle bird told me . . . .

What did the parrot say when it wanted a frog?

*"Polly wants a croaker."*

What did the parakeet say when it was hungry?

*"Long time no seed."*

"What is your hobby?"

"I race pigeons."

"Oh! Have you ever beaten any?"

MOTHER PIGEON: It's time you learned to fly. Either you learn or I'll tie a rope to you and tow you.

YOUNG PIGEON: No, no, not that. I don't want to be pigeon-towed!

# 2. Hiya, Honey!

What do bees call their spouses?

*"Honey."*

When does a B come after U?
*When you disturb its hive.*

Why don't bees have leisure time?

*They're always buzzy.*

Why did the bee join the rock band?
*To be the lead stinger.*

What do bees say on warm days?
*"Swarm, isn't it?"*

What do you call a store owned by a bee?
*A buzziness.*

How do bees brush their hair?
*With honeycombs.*

What did the bee say to the flower?
*"Hey, bud, what time do you open?"*

What did the flower say to the bee?
*"Buzz off."*

If a bee married a rodent, what would their children be called?

*Brats.*

"Ouch! I've just been stung by a bee!"

"Better put something on it."

"Too late. It flew away."

Why did the bee go to the doctor?

*It had hives.*

# 3. Moo-ving Right Along

How do cows cut the grass?
*They moo it.*

What gives milk and has two wheels?

*A cow on a motorcycle.*

Why did the cow cross the street?

*To get to the udder side.*

What happened when the cow jumped over the barbed-wire fence?

*Udder disaster.*

What did the mama cow say to the baby cow?

*"It's pasture bedtime."*

What would you get if you crossed a kangaroo with a cow?

*A kangamoo.*

Knock-Knock.

Who's there?

Cows.

Cows who?

No, cows moo.

What do you call a nervous cow?
*Beef jerky.*

Why does a milking stool have only three legs?
*The cow has the udder one.*

What would you get if you crossed a cow and an octopus?
*A farm animal that milks itself.*

"Are you milking that cow in your new hat?"
*"No, I'm using a pail."*

Knock-Knock.
Who's there?
Europa.
Europa who?
Europa steer and I'll watch.

Why did the cowboy ride his horse to town?

*Because it was too heavy to carry.*

Why did the businessman buy a herd of cattle?

*His future was at steak.*

How do cattlemen plan for the future?
*They make long-range plans.*

Why do cowboys ride in rodcos?
*They like the extra bucks.*

Why did the cowboy go to the rodeo?
*Because wild horses couldn't keep him away.*

"Doctor, ever since I've been riding in the rodeo, I haven't been feeling good. What do you think it could be?"

"Bronc-itis."

Why was the bull's credit card canceled?

*He wouldn't stop charging.*

Where does a bull keep his business papers?

*In his beef case.*

What do cowboys put on their pancakes?

*Maple stirrup.*

Why do cowboys turn their hats up on the side?

*So that three of them can sit in the front in a pickup.*

"Jake, why are you dragging that rope?"

"Have you ever tried pushing one?"

CITY SLICKER: What do you use that rope for?

COWBOY: To catch cattle.

CITY SLICKER: Oh, really? What do you use for bait?

Knock-Knock.

    Who's there?

Donna.

    Donna who?

Donna put the cart before the horse.

Where do horses stay in a hotel?
*In the bridle suite.*

Why did the horse put on the blanket?
*He was a little colt.*

What story is told by a small horse?
*A pony tale.*

What do you call a pony that doesn't whinny?
*A little hoarse.*

What public opinion poll do horses like best?
*The Gallop Poll.*

What do stallions use to fly?
*Horse feathers.*

What do horses put on their salad?
*Mayo-neighs.*

Why couldn't the horse draw the cart?
*He couldn't hold a pencil.*

RIDING INSTRUCTOR: What kind of saddle do you want on your horse – one with a horn or without?

RIDER: Without. There doesn't seem to be much traffic around here.

What did the horse say after finishing its hay?

*"That's the last straw!"*

# 5. Lions and Tigers and Bears

Where does a lion work out?

*At the jungle gym.*

Why do leopards have spotted coats?
*Because the tigers bought all the striped ones.*

Why is it hard to find a store that will sell leopards coats?
*No one wants to wait on them.*

Why did the lion cross the road?
*To get to the other pride.*

What road do lions hang out on?
*Mane Street.*

What do lions and tigers prey on?
*Their knees.*

What would you get if you crossed a lion and a porcupine?

*Something you wouldn't want to sit next to on the bus.*

What would you get if you crossed a white bear and a rabbit?

*A polar hare.*

Can polar bears see in a blizzard?

*Of course. They have great ice sight.*

What is the best way to hunt bear?
*With your clothes off.*

What time is it when a bear comes to dinner?
*Time to go.*

Why couldn't the three bears get back into their house?

*Because it had Goldie locks.*

How do you make bears listen?

*Take away their B's and they are all ears.*

"See that bear rug? That bear was only six feet away. It was either him or me."

"Well, the bear certainly makes a better rug..."

"Did you hear about the hunter who had an accident?"

"No, what happened?"

"It seems he saw some tracks. He went to study them closely. That's when the train hit him."

What does a ghost use to go hunting?

*A boo and arrow.*

Why do bears have fur?

*So their underwear won't show.*

What kind of soda do Australian bears drink?

*Coca-koala.*

Knock-Knock.

Who's there?

Safari.

Safari who?

Safari so good.

TEACHER: Now if you bought ten apples
for ten cents, what would each one be?

SUZY: Rotten. At that price, they'd have to
be.

What does a skunk do before going to school?

*Puts on its stinking cap.*

TEACHER: Gaby, why are you late for school?

GABY: I must have over-washed.

TEACHER: Why are you late for school?

ARLENE: I couldn't help it. School started before I got here.

Knock-Knock.
  Who's there?
Eisenhower.
  Eisenhower who?
Eisenhower late for school.

Knock-Knock.

Who's there?

Goat.

Goat who?

Goat up on the wrong side of the bed.

Why did the worm oversleep?

*It didn't want to get caught by the early bird.*

What's the most disgusting unit of measurement?

*Gross.*

Why did the clock get kicked out of school?

*Because it was always tocking.*

TEACHER: Please answer when I call your name – John Martin.

WILLY: Absent.

TEACHER: Please, Willy, let John answer for himself.

How did the magician make the blackboard disappear?

*Slate of hand.*

TEACHER: This is the worst homework you've ever done, Jane.

JANE: So, now you can't even trust your parents.

MOTHER: The hardest assignment I ever had was to write an essay on the belly of a frog.

DAUGHTER: Wow, how'd you get the frog in the typewriter?

TEACHER: Do you know what an echo is?

JOHNNY: Could you repeat the question?

Why was the little bird punished at school?

*It was caught peeping during a test.*

What kind of test is the most irritating?

*The cross examination.*

What do good students eat their burgers on?

*Honor rolls.*

What's the favorite subject at the South Pole?

*Penguinship.*

Why did the Fig Newton graduate first in his class?

*He was one smart cookie.*

TEACHER: What are the last words of the Gettysburg Address?

JOEY: Er – do you mean the zip code?

TEACHER: Edward, you get a "C" on your exam. What does that mean to you?

EDWARD: Congratulations.

PRINCIPAL: Young man, you are different from the rest of the class.

YOUNG MAN: Really?

PRINCIPAL: Yes, they're graduating.

What did the boy say to the insect?

*"Bug off."*

What do you call a female bug?
  *A gallant.*

What do you call a male bug that floats?

*A buoyant.*

Why was the baby ant so confused?

*Because all of his uncles were ants.*

What do you call a rabbit that is owned by a beetle?

*A bug's bunny.*

Who are the most faithful insects?

*Ticks. Once they find a friend, they stick to him.*

What kind of messages do you get from a bug?

*Flea-mail.*

How do fleas travel?
*They itch-hike.*

What would you get if you crossed a clumsy insect and a grasshopper?
*A clodhopper.*

Knock-Knock.

Who's there?

Flea.

Flea who?

Flea, fie, fo, fum!

What do you call a fly with no wings?

*A walk.*

What did the top fly do when the others didn't do their work?

*Fireflies.*

What do you do when flies come to your picnic?

*Call in the S.W.A.T. team.*

What did one lightning bug say to the other?

"*Give me a push. I think my battery's dead.*"

What do you call a whale that talks too much?

*A blubber mouth.*

Why did the peanut butter jump into the ocean?

*To be with the jellyfish.*

What do you call a man who washes whales?

*A blubber scrubber.*

What's black and white and green?

*A seasick penguin.*

How do oceans make popcorn?

*By microwave.*

Who is the leader of the popcorn?

*The kernel.*

What do you use to cut through the ocean waves?

*A sea-saw.*

What does the Jaws candy bar cost?
*An arm and a leg.*

What would you get if you threw Daffy Duck into the Atlantic Ocean?

*Saltwater Daffy.*


What do you call a lamb that fights on the ocean?

*A battlesheep.*


What city do sharks come from?

*Shark-ago.*


Why did the shark spit out the clown?

*He tasted funny.*


"Did you know that Eskimos once used fish for money?"

"Gee, I bet they had a hard time getting a can of soda out of the machine."

What do you call a fish without an eye?
*A fsh.*

Where does Albert Einstein keep his fish?
*In a think tank.*

Have you ever seen a fish cry?
*No, but I've seen a whale blubber.*

What is a fish's favorite dessert?
*Crab cake.*

Who grants fishes' wishes?
*Their fairy codmother.*

Why don't fish use computers?
*They might get caught in the Net.*

What famous fish wears a red, white, and blue hat?

*Uncle Salmon.*

Who do fish get to clean their rooms?

*Mermaids.*

What are the strongest shellfish in the ocean?

*Mussels.*

Why do salmon swim upstream to spawn?
*Because walking on the riverbank hurts their tails.*

What's big, lives near the beach, and wears sunglasses?
*A two-hundred-pound seagull.*

What do you call a beach that keeps losing sand?
*A shore loser.*

"Is that a surfboard?"

"No, it's a tongue depressor for my pet shark."

What's the best way to get around on the ocean floor?
*By taxi crab.*

Where do fish wash themselves?

*In bass-tubs.*

POLICEMAN: Hey, you! What are you doing walking down the street with a desk on your back?

MAN: I'm impersonating an office, sir.

When do you go on red and stop on green?

*When you're eating watermelon.*

Why did the policeman put handcuffs on the front door of a home?

*He was making a house arrest.*

POLICEMAN: Do you know that's a stolen car you're driving?

DRIVER: Of course I do. How do you think I got it?

"Did you hear that the police caught a workaholic?"

"What was he charged with?"

"He was resisting a rest."

What organized gang destroys wool coats?

*The Mothia.*

DIT: The police are looking for a man with one eye named Smith.

DOT: What's the other eye named?

How do they catch crooks at McDonald's?
*With burger alarms.*

MAN *(to police desk sergeant)*: Someone threw this dead fish into my front yard.

SERGEANT: Okay, sir. Come back in six months and if nobody claims it, you can keep it.

A police station received a call:
  "Someone just stole my truck!"
  "Did you see who it was?"
  "No, but I got the license number."

What is the police officers' favorite board game?
*Monopolice.*

How do you know when a cat burglar has been at your house?

*Your cat is missing.*

JUDGE: Don't you know that crime doesn't pay?

CRIMINAL: Yes, but the hours are good.

JUDGE: You are accused of shooting rabbits out of season. How do you plead?

HUNTER: Self-defense, your honor.

JUDGE: The court can produce a dozen witnesses who saw you rob the bank.

ROBBER: Big deal! I can bring in hundreds of people who didn't see it.

What did the judge do when he sentenced the author?

*He threw the book at him.*

Why did the bar of soap confess?

*It wanted to come clean.*

Where did they send the ink that was found guilty of forgery?

*To the state pen.*

Who stole the soap?

*The robber ducky.*

Did you hear about the thief who robbed the exercise class? He was put away for a long stretch.

What do you call a person who steals rubber bands?

*A rubber bandit.*

JEWELER: Hello, 911? I own a jewelry store and an elephant just walked in, sucked up all my jewelry with his trunk, and ran away.

POLICE: Can you give me a description?

JEWELER: I can't really, because he had a nylon stocking over his head.

"Were you afraid when the robber pulled a knife on you?"

"No, I could see he wasn't a professional. The knife still had butter on it."

Why did the police arrest the cat?

*Because of the kitty litter.*

How many judges does it take to change a light bulb?

*Two. One to turn it and another to overturn it.*

What is a lawyer's favorite meal?
*Brief Stroganoff.*


Where do lawyers play tennis?
*At the Supreme Court.*


POLICEMAN: Your license says you should
be wearing glasses. Why aren't you
wearing them?

MOTORIST: I have contacts.

Policeman: I don't care who you know.
I'm giving you a ticket.


What telephone number does a pig call
when it gets into trouble?
*Swine one one.*

How do hamburgers catch robbers?
  *With a burger alarm.*

GRANDPA: Uh-oh. I just made an illegal
  right turn.
GRANDSON: That's okay, Grandpa. The
  police car behind you did the same
  thing.

Why wasn't the crooked railroad
conductor arrested?
  *Because he covered his tracks.*

"How long will your brother be in jail?"
  "Thirty days."
  "What's the charge?"
  "No charge. Everything's free."

# 10. PLAY BALL!

Why are so many baseball games played at night?

*Because bats sleep during the daytime.*

What do you call a jail that is specially designed for baseball sluggers?

*The Grand Slammer.*

What has 18 legs, catches flies, and has red spots?

*A baseball team with the measles.*

What position does a pig play in baseball?

*Short-slop.*

What would you get if you crossed a lobster with a baseball player?

*A pinch hitter.*

Where do birds play baseball?

*In the mynah leagues.*

From what do catchers eat their dinner?

*Home plate.*

How can you keep cool at the ball park?

*Sit by a fan.*

What word is frowned at by baseball players but smiled at by bowlers?

*"Strike."*

What player on a baseball team pours the lemonade?

*The pitcher.*

What traffic violation is common in baseball?

*Hit and run.*

Knock-Knock.

Who's there?

Michigan.

Michigan who?

"Michigan," said the batter, after the third strike.

Knock-Knock.

Who's there?

Basis.

Basis who?

Basis loaded, nobody out!

BASEBALL COACH: Remember all those batting and fielding tips I gave you?

ROOKIE: I sure do.

COACH: Well, forget them. We traded you.

What's the best place to keep your baseball mitt?

*In the glove compartment.*

What did the baseball glove say to the baseball?

*"Catch you later."*

# 11. WHICH CAME FIRST?

What size T-shirt do you buy for a 200-pound egg?

*Eggs-tra large.*

What did the chicken say when she laid a square egg?

*"Ouch!"*

What was the nearsighted chicken doing in the billiard parlor?

*Trying to hatch the cue ball.*

What does an egg do when another egg bothers it?

*Eggnores it.*

Why was the hen so arrogant?

*She had a large eggo.*

What egg is dangerous?

*The eggsecutioner.*

What does Tinker Bell use to fry eggs?

*A Peter Pan.*

What do you call an omelet your mother makes for you?

*A momelet.*

Why are chickens such big eaters?
  *Because they eat a peck at a time.*

Knock-Knock.

   Who's there?

Rook.

   Rook who?

Rook out – the sky is falling!

How does the beach like its eggs?
*Sunny side up.*

How does a comedian like his eggs?
*Funny side up.*

What do people call chickens in prison?
*Henmates.*

What would you get if you crossed a
chicken with a bicycle?
*A hen-speed bike.*

Why didn't the omelet laugh?
*It didn't get the yolk.*

Knock-Knock.

Who's there?

Lass.

Lass who?

Lass one out is a rotten egg.

What did the duck say when she bought lipstick?

*"Just put it on my bill."*

What is a duck's favorite snack?

*Quacker Jacks.*

If a duck says "Quack, quack" when it walks, what does it say when it runs?

*"Quick, quick!"*

If people live in condos, where do ducks live?

*In pondos.*

How do you heal a broken duck?

*Use duck tape.*

What do you call someone who treats sick ducks?

*A ducktor.*

# 12. ELEPHANT SECRETS

What do elephants wear on their legs?
  *Elepants.*

Why don't elephants play basketball?

*They don't look good in shorts.*

Why are elephant rides cheaper than pony rides?

*Elephants work for peanuts.*

Why does an elephant need a trunk?

*So it has something to hide behind when it sees a mouse.*

Who gives money to elephants who lose a tooth?

*The Tusk Fairy.*

Why do elephants have round feet?

*So they can walk on lily pads.*

Why do elephants have cracks between their toes?

*To carry their library cards.*

Why do elephants prefer peanuts to chocolate mousse?

*Peanuts are easier to get at the ballpark.*

What elephant flies?

*A Dumbo jet.*

What weighs 12,000 pounds and is covered
with special sauce?
*A Big MacElephant.*

What's convenient and weighs two tons?
*An elephant six-pack.*

Why don't elephants tip bellhops?
*They like to carry their own trunks.*

Why do elephants have trunks?
*Because they can't carry all their stuff
in their makeup case.*

What would you get if you put 100 pounds
of peanuts in an elephant's cage?
*A happy elephant.*

How can you tell if an elephant is in your cereal box?

*Read the label.*

How can you tell that an elephant is on your head during a hurricane?

*You hear his ears flapping in the wind.*

How can you tell that an elephant is living in your house?

*By the enormous pajamas in your closet.*

How can you tell an elephant from a banana?

*Try lifting it. If you can't get it off the ground, it's probably an elephant. Although it might be a heavy banana.*

What goes clunk-clunk, squash-squash, clunk-clunk?

*An elephant with wet sneakers.*

"Do elephants know how to gamble?"

"I don't have the Vegas idea."

How can you tell if an elephant has been using your toothbrush?

*It smells like peanuts.*

Why did the elephant walk around in white socks?

*Someone stole its running shoes.*

What would you get if you crossed an elephant and an alligator?

*An elephator.*

"More than 50,000 elephants go each year to make piano keys."

"Really? It's amazing what animals can be trained to do!"

Why did the elephants laugh at Tarzan?
*They thought his nose was funny.*

# 13. SHOP TILL YOU DROP

Knock-Knock.

Who's there?

Castor.

Castor who?

Castor pearls before swine.

CUSTOMER: Look at that watch you sold me. It broke. You told me it would last a lifetime.

CLERK: Yes, but you looked pretty sick the day you bought it.

Where does a lumberjack go to buy things?
*To the chopping center.*

Where do spies do their shopping?
*At a snooper market.*

Where do bugs buy their groceries?
*At the flea market.*

Why do most cities have the same stores?
*It's a mall world.*

"I was at the mall yesterday on an escalator and there was a power failure."
"So?"
"I was stuck for hours."

ANGRY CUSTOMER: Those safety matches you sold me won't strike.

STOREKEEPER: Well, you can't get much safer than that.


APPLIANCE STORE CLERK: May I interest you in a new freezer?

LADY: No, I can't afford it.

CLERK: It will pay for itself in no time.

LADY: Okay, as soon as it does, send it over.


LADY *(in pet shop)*: Have you got any kittens going cheap?

PET SHOP OWNER: No, ma'am, all our kittens go "meow."

BOY: Mister, could you sell me a shark?

PET SHOP OWNER: What do you want
with a shark?

BOY: My cat's trying to eat my goldfish,
and I want to teach him a lesson.

CUSTOMER: Four bars of soap, please.

CLERK: Scented?

CUSTOMER: No, I'll take them with me.

CUSTOMER: I'd like a pair of stockings for my wife.

CLERK: Sheer?

CUSTOMER: No, she's home.

What's a caveman's favorite place to shop?
*Cave Mart.*

"I have this terrible problem. Whenever I go shopping, I buy everything that is marked down."

"Why is that a problem?"

"Last week I bought an escalator."

Why do deer use discount coupons?
*They like to save big bucks and lots of doe.*

Why did the actress go the bakery?
*She was looking for good roles.*

Why did the frankfurter bun turn down offers from Hollywood?
*The rolls weren't good enough.*

What's the best way to buy holes?
*Wholesale.*

**SIGN LANGUAGE**
Convenience Store: WE'LL SERVE YOU
FAST NO MATTER HOW LONG IT TAKES.

What do you say when you walk into a
store at the same time as a sheep?

*"After ewe."*

# 14. FUNKY FAMILIES

BIFF: Do you have a family tree?

CLIFF: No, we don't even have a flowerpot.

What pen does a baby write with?
   *A play pen.*

"When I was a child, my nurse dropped me a lot."

   "What did your mother do?"

   "She got me a shorter nurse."

Knock-Knock.

Who's there?

Mustard.

Mustard who?

Mustard been a beautiful baby.


Why was Little Miss Muffet upset?

*She didn't get her whey.*


What do you call a fast tricycle?

*A tot rod.*


"Are you sure your mother won't mind me sailing my boat in your bathtub?"

"No, she can always slide over to the other side."

Knock-Knock.

Who's there?

Dwayne.

Dwayne who?

Dwayne the bathtub – I'm dwowning.


DOCTOR: Congratulations! You're the father of twins!

MAN: Don't tell my wife. I want to surprise her.


FATHER: We have twins at our house.

NEIGHBOR: Are they identical?

FATHER: One is and one isn't.

BOY: Mom, Uncle Charlie took me to the zoo this afternoon.

MOTHER: That's nice. Did you have a good time?

BOY: Yes, and one of the animals came in first and paid twenty dollars.

"My brother is in the hospital with spotted fever."

"Is it serious?"

"No, fortunately they spotted it in time."

Where do old bicycles go?
*To the old spokes' home.*

"I married a girl who is a twin."

"How can you tell them apart?"

"Her brother has a beard."

DAD: There's something wrong with my toothbrush.

SON: That's funny. It was all right when I used it to oil my bike chain.

DAD: Sonny, why did you let the air out of the tires on your bike?

SONNY: So I could reach the pedals.

MOTHER: Drink your milk, dear, it makes strong teeth.

COOKIE: Why don't you give some to Grandpa?

"Mom, you know that vase that's
been handed down from generation to
generation?"

"Yes?"

"Well, this generation dropped it."

"I'd like to talk with your mother, young man. Is she engaged?"

"Engaged? She's married."

FATHER: What is the meaning of all these Ds and Fs on your report card?

CHARLIE: That means I'm Doing Fine.

MOTHER: You know, you're not supposed to eat peas with your knife.

JUNIOR: I know, but my fork leaks.

MOTHER: You look pretty dirty, Son.

SON: Gee, Mom, I thought I looked better clean.

"Your big sister is spoiled, isn't she?"

"No, that's just the perfume she's wearing."

LITTLE ARTHUR: Mom, my sister went and
    backed the car over my bicycle again.
MOM: Is that right?
BIG SISTER: Yes, but it's his own fault. He
    shouldn't have left it in the kitchen.

"How come you're wearing your brother's
raincoat?"

    "I don't want to get his new sweater wet."

Who is the Pied Piper's poor brother?
    *The Pied Pauper.*

Do robots have brothers?
    *No, they have trans-sisters.*

What do you call a llama's mother?
    *A mama llama.*

WOMAN: Do you have any grandchildren?
ELDERLY WOMAN: No, all my children are
    ordinary.

What award do singing grandmothers get?
*Grammies.*

A college student wrote his father a note
that said:
*No money.*
*Not funny.*
*Love, Sonny.*
His father wrote
back:
*So sad.*
*Too bad.*
*Love, Dad.*

"Where can I get hold of your sister?"
"I don't know. She's awfully ticklish."

"I hear your brother fell into an upholstery machine."

"Yes, but he's fully recovered now."

"Did you know my robot can walk?"

"That's nothing. My refrigerator can run."

"My grandma fell down the stairs."

"Cellar?"

"No, I think she can be repaired."

What did the mother rope say to her child?

*"Don't be knotty."*

MOM: For once I'd like to come into the kitchen and not see you digging through the refrigerator.

KID: Try whistling before you come in.

MOTHER: Did I make the toast too dark?

DAUGHTER: I can't tell yet. The smoke is too thick.

GRANDMA: Remember my motto. Never put off till tomorrow what you can do today.

GRANDDAUGHTER: Okay, Grandma, that makes sense. We'd better eat the rest of the cake.

Why is it hard to be a turtle?

*You can't run away from home.*

What do you say to a boomerang on its birthday?

*"Many happy returns."*

# 15. ON THE ROAD

TAXI DRIVER: I can't stop this car! I've lost control!

PASSENGER: For heaven's sake, turn off the meter!

It takes a thousand nuts and bolts to put a car together, but just one nut to scatter it all over the road.

"I know a guy who stole parts from ten different cars and put them all together."

"What did he get?"

"Twenty years."

Why did the fisherman destroy his polluted car?

*His Mercury was filled with tuna.*

HIGHWAY PATROLMAN: You were going seventy miles per hour.

SPEEDER: I was only following the signs.

PATROLMAN: That's the number of the highway.

SPEEDER: It is? I'm glad you didn't stop me on I-95.


SPEEDER: I didn't hear your siren.

OFFICER: Of course not. You already passed the sound barrier.


TRAFFIC COP: This is a ticket for speeding.

DRIVER: Oh, thank you. When do I get to use it?


How much do used batteries cost?
*Nothing, they are free of charge.*

Did you hear about the tire that had a nervous breakdown? It couldn't take the pressure.

What has five horns, four wheels, and weighs ten tons?

*Four rhinos in a convertible.*

POLICEMAN: Let me see your license. Did you know you were speeding?

DRIVER: But, Officer, I was only trying to keep a safe distance between my car and the car in back of me.

Spotting a woman knitting while she was driving, a motorcycle patrolman pulled alongside of her car and shouted, "Pull over!"

"No, silly," called the lady. "It's a pair of mittens."

What would you get if you crossed a jaguar and an elephant?

*A sports car with a big trunk.*

"It's outrageous that this truck driver is charging us $50 for towing us two miles."

"Don't worry. He's earning it. I have the brakes on."

SON: Dad, I have some good news and some bad news.

FATHER: Okay, give me the good news first.

SON: I drove the car this morning, and I'm happy to report that the air bag works great.

CUSTOMER: I've come to buy a car, but I don't remember the name. It starts with "T".

SALESMAN: Sorry, we don't have cars that start with tea. All our cars start with gasoline.

**SIGN LANGUAGE**

**Sign in a muffler shop:** NO APPOINTMENT NECESSARY. WE HEARD YOU COMING.

MOTORIST: How far is it to the next town?

FARMER: Two miles, as the crow flies.

MOTORIST: How far is it if the crow has to roll a flat tire?

What is Mickey Mouse's favorite car?
*A Minnie van.*

"This is a magic car," said the man, as he gave his daughter the keys.

"Really?" said the girl.

"Yes," said her father. "One speeding ticket and it will disappear."

What makes sheep such bad drivers?
*They make too many ewe turns.*

What driver never gets a ticket?
*A screwdriver.*

"Do you know I can read bumper stickers on cars going 55 miles per hour?"

"No kidding."

"Yeah, I took a speed-reading course."

DRIVER *(on cell phone)*: Help! My car is stuck in quicksand!

INSURANCE AGENT: Don't get excited!

DRIVER: Why not?

INSURANCE AGENT: Because your car will be completely covered.

What car breathes fire?
*A station dragon.*

What car does an electrician drive?
*A Voltswagen.*

What vehicle does a hog drive?
*A pig-up truck.*

What do you call pigs that drive trucks?
*Squeals on wheels.*

From what kind of dish does a car eat?

*A license plate.*

Why was the car embarrassed?

*It had gas.*

How is an old car like a baby?

*It never goes anywhere without a rattle.*

Why do people park in a driveway and drive on a parkway?

Do truck drivers have tough jobs?

*Yes, they have many bumps on the road.*

Why did the truck driver's wife divorce him?

*He drove her up the wall.*

When does a truck driver stop to eat?

*When he comes to a fork in the road.*

What was the tow truck doing at the race track?

*Trying to pull a fast one.*

How do you get a frog off the back window of your car?

*Use the rear defrogger.*

CAB DRIVER: Lady, that 25-cent tip you gave me was an insult.

LADY: How much should I tip you?

CAB DRIVER: Another 25 cents.

LADY: What? And insult you twice?

Did you hear about the new car that runs on peanut butter? It gets good mileage but sticks to the roof of your garage.

# 16. CATS AND DOGS

What magazine do cats like to read?
*Good Mousekeeping.*

What cat likes to go bowling?

*An alley cat.*

Why did the cat put its kittens into a drawer?

*It didn't want to leave its litter lying around.*

WIFE: Why didn't you get the cat fixed?
HUSBAND: It wasn't broken.

"Junior, don't pull the cat's tail."
  "I'm only holding it. The cat is pulling it."

What do hurt cats say?
  *"Me-OWW!"*

What's a cat's favorite dessert?
  *Chocolate mouse.*

How do you get milk from a cat?
  *Steal its saucer.*

What do cats call mice on rollerskates?
  *Meals on wheels.*

What would you get if you crossed a plump cat with a duck?

*A duck-filled fatty puss.*

What do cats like on a hot day?

*A mice cream cone.*

Knock-Knock.

  Who's there?

Violet.

  Violet who?

Violet the cat out of the bag?

What would you get if you crossed a shark with a cat?

*A town without dogs.*

Knock-Knock.
  Who's there?
Defense.
  Defense who?
Defense keeps the dog in.

Did you hear about the man who was so grouchy that his dog put up a sign that said "BEWARE OF OWNER"?

What would you get if you crossed a newt and a poodle?

*A newdle.*

What do you do when your dog has ticks?
  *Don't wind him.*

MAN: Have you got something to cure fleas on a dog?

PET SHOP OWNER: I don't know. What's wrong with the fleas?

BARRY: Does your dog have a license?

LARRY: No, I don't let him drive.

"Did you tell me your dog's bark is worse than his bite?"

"Yes, why?"

"Then don't let him bark – he just bit me."

Why do fire trucks have dogs on them?

*To find the fire hydrant.*

What dog bakes cakes?

*Betty Cocker.*

POLICE OFFICER: You are charged with having your dog chase a man on a bicycle.

MAN: That's crazy. My dog doesn't even know how to ride a bicycle.

What would you get if you crossed a pit bull with Lassie?

*A dog that bites your leg off and then runs for help.*

"I've got a slow dog."

"How can you tell?"

"This morning he brought me yesterday's newspaper."

"What does a dog say when it gets sick?"

"Barf! Barf!"

"And what does it say when it sits on sandpaper?"

"Ruff! Ruff!"

"Has your dog a pedigree?"

"Has she! If she could talk, she wouldn't speak to either of us."

How are dogcatchers paid?

*By the pound.*

What did the boy say when his puppy ran away from home?

*"Doggone!"*

MAN: Are you sure this dog you're selling me is loyal?

OWNER: He sure is. I've sold him five times and every time he's come back.

"My dog is going to obedience school."

"That's expensive. How can you afford it?"

"He won a collarship."

"How do you like my new dog?"

"Spitz?"

"No, but he drools a lot."

Why did the Dalmatian go to the dry cleaners?

*His coat had spots all over it.*

What kind of arguments do dogs like at dinner?

*Table scraps.*

What two dogs are opposites?

*Hot dogs and chili dogs.*

What does a dog do that a person steps in?

*Pants.*

If every dog has his day, what does a dog with a broken tail have?

*A weekend.*

Who brings dogs their presents at Christmas?

*Santa Paws.*

What kind of dog washes clothes?

*A laundro-mutt.*

What has no hair and thinks it's the national dog of the United States?

*The bald beagle.*

Knock-Knock.

Who's there?

Beagle.

Beagle who?

Beagle with cream cheese.

What's a dog's favorite soup?

*Chicken poodle.*

What do you call the top of a doghouse?
*The woof.*

Why do puppies eat frankfurters?
*Because it's a dog-eat-dog world.*

What are the three reasons people have dogs for pets?
*Hyenas are too noisy, elephants can't fit through the front door, and you can't walk a fish on a leash.*

Knock-Knock.
Who's there?
Detail.
Detail who?
Detail is wagging the dog.

"I used to think I was a dog, but the doctor cured me."

"So, you're all right now?"

"Yes, here – feel my nose."

# 17. ALL DECKED OUT

Knock-Knock.
   Who's there?
Coburn.
   Coburn who?
Coburn your clothes!

"I'd like to buy a pair of thermal underwear."

"How long do you want them?"

"From October to March."

"What should I wear with my new tie?"

"A long beard."

CUSTOMER: Look at this coat you sold me! It split up the back!

SALESMAN: That shows how tightly the buttons were sewn on.

MOTHER: Did you fall down with your good pants on?

SON: Yes. I didn't have time to take them off.

"Did you knit this sweater all by yourself?"

"Yes, all except the hole you put your head through. That was there when I started."

What did the tailor say to the customer?
*"Suit yourself."*

What's the best pattern for a baker's suit?
*Checks.*

Knock-Knock.
Who's there?
Cypress.
Cypress who?
Cypress your suit?

Knock-Knock.
Who's there?
Dakota.
Dakota who?
Dakota fits fine, but the pants are too long.

**154**

What did the zero say to the eight?

*"Nice belt."*

How did the belt break the law?

*It held up a pair of pants.*

What did they wear at the Boston Tea Party?

*T-shirts.*

What's the best shirt to wear into battle?

*A tank top.*

Why did the girl protest being expelled for wearing a tank top?

*She wanted to the right to bare arms.*

What do you call a near-collision of two dresses?

*A clothes call.*

Knock-Knock.
Who's there?
Eugenes.
Eugenes who?
Eugenes need washing.

Knock-Knock.
Who's there?
Dispense.
Dispense who?
Dispense are too tight.

# 18. GOING WILD!

What do you call a dinosaur that's never late?

*Prontosaurus.*

Knock-Knock.

Who's there?

Dinosaur.

Dinosaur who?

Dinosaur at you – you burnt the toast.

What's gray on the inside and brown on the outside?

*A chocolate-covered dinosaur.*

What dinosaur coughs the most?

*The bronchitis.*

Who saw the stegosaurus enter the restaurant?

*The diners saw.*

Why is a dinosaur healthier than a dragon?

*Because a dinosaur doesn't smoke.*

What's a tired kangaroo?

*Out of bounds.*

What do you call a lazy baby kangaroo?

*A pouch potato.*

What would you get if you crossed a kangaroo with a snake?

*A jump rope.*

What's long and poisonous and tells on you?

*A tattlesnake.*

How do snakes eat so well with no hands?

*They have forked tongues.*

What would you get if you crossed pasta with a boa constrictor?

*Spaghetti that winds itself around the fork.*

Why did the snake lose its lawsuit?

*It didn't have a leg to stand on.*

What would you get if you crossed a
magician with a snake?

*Abra-ca-cobra.*

How do snakes sign their letters?

*"Love and hisses."*

What did the viper do when she had a cold?

*Viped her nose.*

What did the girl snake give the boy snake
after their first date?

*A good-night hiss.*

FIRST SNAKE: I'm writing my hiss-tory.
SECOND SNAKE: I'm a writer, too. I write
boa-graphies.

What's black and white and very
dangerous?

*A zebra on a skateboard.*

What's black and white and wet all over?

*A zebra taking a shower.*

What's black and white and green?

*A seasick zebra.*

What did the silly man name his pet zebra?

*Spot.*


Where do Arabs leave their camels when they go shopping?

*In a camelot.*


What kind of animal puts other creatures into a trance?

*The hypno-potamus.*


Why did the hippo stop using soap?

*Because it left a ring around the river.*


What hippo never stops eating?

*A hippobottomless.*

What jungle animal is always pouting?
  *A whinoceros.*

What did the monkey say to the vine?
  *"Okay if I hang around?"*

What goes "Ouch, ouch, ouch, ouch, ouch, ouch, ouch, ouch . . ."?

*An octopus with tight shoes.*

What has eight arms and four wheels?

*An octo-bus.*

Why do giraffes make good friends?
  *They really stick their necks out for you.*

What's worse than a giraffe with a sore throat?

  *An octopus with tennis elbow.*

What would you get if you crossed a
beagle with a giraffe?

*A dog that barks at airplanes.*

# 19. WORKING OVERTIME

Knock-Knock.
  Who's there?
Barber.
  Barber who?
Barber, black sheep.

What do you want to be when you grow up?

*Taller.*


Why did the guy use the daily paper for Kleenex?

*He had a nose for news.*


Why did the reporter buy an ice cream cone?

*He was desperate for a scoop.*


A young man applied for a summer job.

"The job," said the employer, "is for a garbage collector. Do you have any experience?"

"No, sir," said the young man. "But I can pick it up as I go along."

FOREMAN: Come on, get a move on with that bricklaying.

BRICKLAYER: Rome wasn't built in a day, you know.

FOREMAN: That's because I wasn't the foreman on the job.

"I got a new job restoring antiques."

"That's interesting. Where do you work?"

"At the beauty clinic."

What did the rabbit think of the job offer?
*She thought it was a real hopper-tunity.*

How do you fool a sheep?
*You pull the wool over its eyes.*

"Are you typing any faster these days?"
*"Yep. I'm up to ten mistakes a minute."*

What mistake do you keep making – that you know you've made before?
*A déjà boo-boo.*

A man was taking a test to be a letter carrier. The first question was: "How far is it from the earth to the moon?"

"Look," he said, "if that's going to be my route, forget it."

A man filling out a job application came to the part in the form that said, "List the person to notify in case of an emergency."

The man thought and then wrote, "First person you see."

BOSS: I've got to hire a new chauffeur. He nearly killed me today.
WORKER: Oh, give him another chance.

In what factory does Humpty Dumpty work?
*In an eggplant.*

What happened when all the king's men told Humpty Dumpty a joke?
*He fell for it.*

Why did the watchman get a promotion?

*He worked 'round the clock.*

What do you call a plumber's helper?

*A drainee.*

A plumber went to the house of a customer.

"I'm sorry I'm a few days late to fix the leak in your basement," the plumber said.

"Oh, the time wasn't totally wasted," replied the wet customer. "Since I called you, I taught my daughter to swim."

A man got a job painting the white line on the middle of the highway. After three days the foreman called him in for a talk.

"The first day on the job you painted five miles of highway, the second day one mile, and today you only painted 100 feet. How come you're slowing down like that?"

"Can't be helped," replied the man. "I keep getting farther and farther away from the can."

Boss: How is it that every time I come around you're not working?

Worker: You wear sneakers.


Why was the lumberjack so successful?

*Don't ax.*


What's a lumberjack's favorite month?

*Sep-tiiiiimberrrrrr!*


Why couldn't the lumberjack keep up with his work?

*He was backlogged.*


What sign do you put on the top of a dummy's ladder?

*"STOP!"*

Knock-Knock.

Who's there?

Macon.

Macon who?

Macon a mountain out of a molehill.

How did the laundry woman look after a day's work?

*Washed out.*

## BOOKS NEVER WRITTEN

*Getting Places on Time* by Harriet Upp.

*I Was a Double Agent* by S.P.N. Hodge.

*How to Be a Basketball Player*
   by Duncan Pass.

*How to Get out of Debt*
   by I.O.A. Bundle.

*Inside a Garbage Truck*
   by Howie Voltan.

*How to Be a Weight Lifter*
   by Buster Gutt.

*Fast Food Franchises* by Eaton Run.

How did the ditchdigger get his job?

*He fell into it.*

How do you confuse a ditchdigger?

*Hand him two shovels and tell him to take his pick.*

What works best when it has something in its eye?

*A sewing needle.*

How does a tailor work out?

*On a thread mill.*

How can you tell when a tailor is going crazy?

*He starts coming apart at the seams.*

How was the tailor after the accident?
*On the mend.*

How did the man do in his new job selling shoes?
*He got off on the wrong foot.*

How did the firefighter quit his job?
*In the heat of the moment.*

Why did the plumber quit his job?
*He found it draining.*

Why was the mortician fired?
*He couldn't meet his deadlines.*

Why was the auto parts salesman fired?
*He took too many brakes.*

Why was Count Dracula fired?

*He made a few grave errors.*

Why was the man fired from the M&M factory?

*He threw away all the Ws.*


What happened to the human cannonball at the circus?

*He was hired and fired on the same day.*


How did the tailor do in the stock market?

*He lost his shirt.*


What do you call it when a police officer quits?

*A cop out.*


Why did the railroad conductor return to his old job?

*He wanted to get back on track.*

Why did the gardener quit his job?

*He didn't like the celery.*

How did the gardener feel at the end of the day?

*Bushed.*

How do canaries earn extra money?

*They babysit for elephants on Saturday night.*

What happens when a Finnish swimmer gets into trouble?

*Helsinki.*

# 20. BODY PARTS

When is an arm dangerous?

*When it's a firearm.*

"What happened to your finger?"

"I was trying out my new hammer and hit the wrong nail."

What did the mitten say to the thumb?

*"I glove you."*

What part of the body is a real loser?

*Defeat.*

If the palm of your hand itches, you're about to get something. If your head itches, you've got it.

If an athlete gets athlete's foot, what does a scuba diver get?

*Under toe.*

"Why don't you wash your neck?"
   "Then it wouldn't match my sneakers."

What should you do when your ear rings?
   *Answer it.*

What do insurance companies pay you when you get a bump on your head?
   *A lump sum.*

How do you keep a stiff upper lip?
   *Put starch in your mustache.*

What part of a letter carrier's anatomy is the first to go?
   *Deliver.*

Knock-Knock.

  Who's there?

Tacoma.

  Tacoma who?

Tacoma your hair – it's a mess.

What did one knee bone say to the other knee bone?

*"Let's get out of this joint."*

What are goose bumps for?

*To keep geese from speeding.*

What are hippies for?

*To keep your leggies up.*

Did you hear they found the gene for shyness?

*It was hiding behind some other genes.*

"In your opinion, what is the height of stupidity?"

"How tall are you?"

What happened when a hundred hares got loose on Main Street?

*The police had to comb the area.*

Knock-Knock.

 Who's there?

Lightning.

 Lightning who?

Lightning your hair, my dear?

What do hairdressers do at the end of their lives?

*They curl up and dye.*

What do you call an attack by a bunch of wigs?

*A hair raid.*

Was the man wearing his toupee in the wrong place?

*Yes, they pulled the rug out from under him.*

How does a wig introduce itself?

*"Hair I am!"*

PATIENT: Doctor, I just swallowed a bone!
DOCTOR: Are you choking?
PATIENT: No, I'm serious.

"Be careful with that cold. Sneeze the other way."

"I don't know any other way."

What's the best way to break a bad habit?
*Drop it.*

"I finally got my little brother to stop biting his nails."

"How?"

"I made him wear shoes."

Why do smokers whisper?
*Because smoking is not aloud.*

What should smokers do to quit?
*Butt out.*

# 21. FAVORITE CHARACTERS

What superhero doesn't like to share things?

*Bratman.*

Knock-Knock.

Who's there?

Clark Kent.

Clark Kent who?

Clark Kent come, he's sick.

What's Superman's favorite street?
*Lois Lane.*

What should you do if Lois Lane steals?
*Reporter.*

Who taught Superman to tell time?
*Clock Kent.*

What flies through the air and is covered with syrup?
*Peter Pancake.*

What do you call a supernatural being with a tan-colored rabbit?
*Genie with the light brown hare.*

How did King Kong escape from his cage?

*He used a monkey wrench.*

How did they train King Kong?

*They hit him with a large rolled-up newspaper building.*

What is a pig's favorite tale?

*Slopping Beauty.*

# 22. SUN AND FUN

Why don't fish go away for the summer?
*Because they are always in school.*

What's brown, hairy, and wears sunglasses?

*A coconut on vacation.*

Where do fish go on vacation?

*To Finland.*

Where does a shoe salesman go on vacation?

*Boot camp.*


Knock-Knock.

Who's there?

Fortification.

Fortification who?

Fortification I go to the seashore.


What luggage did the puppy bring on vacation?

*A doggie bag.*


What kind of luggage always makes a fuss?

*Carry-on.*

Where do owls stay when they travel?
*In hoot-els.*

Where do cows stay when they travel?
*Moo-tels.*

BUCK: I went to a hotel for a change and a rest.

CHUCK: Did you get it?

BUCK: No, the bellboy got the change and the hotel got the rest.

"I stopped at a very exclusive hotel."

"How exclusive was it?"

"It was so exclusive that room service had an unlisted number."

"Hello, front desk."

"How much do you charge for a room?"

"Our rates start at $350 a day."

"Do you take children?"

"No, sir, only cash and credit cards."

HOTEL OWNER: I won't charge you for the breakfast because you didn't eat it.

Guest: Thanks. By the way, I didn't sleep last night.

MAN IN HOTEL: Excuse me, but I'm registered at this hotel. Could you tell me what room I'm in?

HOTEL CLERK: Certainly. You're in the lobby.

BOSS: What's this big item on your expense account?

SALESMAN: Oh, that's the hotel bill.

BOSS: Well, don't buy any more hotels.

"I'm always sick before a trip."

"Then why don't you leave a day earlier?"

"My uncle was on a quiz show and won a trip to Australia."

"Did he go?"

"Yes, five years ago. He's been trying to win a trip back ever since."

"My daughter went on a cruise."

"Jamaica?"

"No, she wanted to go."

"My son came to visit me on vacation."

"That's nice. Did you meet him at the airport?"

"No, I've known him all my life."

"Great news, Son! We've saved enough money to go to Disneyland."

"That's great, Dad. When are we going?"

"As soon as we save enough to get back."

What kind of journey can you take without leaving your home?

*An ego trip.*

TRAVELER: Is this the bus to California?

TICKET AGENT: Yes, it goes to California in 10 minutes.

TRAVELER: Wow! That fast!

Which roads are always angry?
*Crossroads.*

"Why are you still standing on the corner? Didn't I tell you to take the 15th Street bus?"

"Sure, but so far only ten have gone by."

TOURIST: What is this necklace made of?

NATIVE: Alligator teeth.

TOURIST: I guess they have the same value as pearls do to my people.

NATIVE: Not quite. Anyone can open an oyster.

Why did the elephant have a terrible vacation?

*The airline lost his trunk.*

TOURIST: Excuse me – how far is it to Smithville?

COUNTRY BOY: It's 5,000 miles in the direction you're heading in your car, but only five miles if you turn around and go the other way.

PASSENGER: Are you sure this train stops at San Francisco?

CONDUCTOR: If it doesn't, you're going to hear an awful splash.

TOURIST: Do you make life-size enlargements from snapshots?

PHOTO CLERK: Yes, that's our specialty.

TOURIST: Here are some pictures of the Grand Canyon.

What did the detective say when he finished packing his suitcase?

*"Case closed."*

How does a gym teacher travel?

*He flies coach.*

Knock-Knock.

Who's there?

Levin.

Levin who?

Levin on a jet plane.

Why did the pony think it could fly?
*Because it saw the horsefly.*

What do you call a bunch of planes that fly backwards?
*A receding airline.*

A flight attendant on an airplane was taking orders. She asked one woman, "Would you like a meal?"

"What are my choices?" asked the woman.

"Yes or no."

"What do you do for a living?"

"I'm a pilot."

"Oh, you fly airplanes?"

"No, I work in an office with lots of paperwork. I pile it here and I pile it there."

Do pilots get cold?

*No, flew.*

What ailment do most pilots experience?

*Soars.*

What plane flies backwards?

*An error plane.*

GROUND RADAR: Enemy at two o'clock!

PILOT: What should I do till then?

"I'm handing out gum before the flight starts," announced the flight attendant. "It will prevent your ears from popping as we climb."

After the flight, everyone left except one man. "Why are you still here?" the flight attendant asked.

"Ah, you have to speak up," yelled the man. "I can't hear you with this gum in my ears."

PILOT *(to passengers)*: I have good news and bad news. The bad news is we're lost.

PASSENGER: What's the good news?

PILOT: We're making good time.


PILOT *(to passengers)*: We have lost one of our engines, so we'll be an hour late for our arrival.

PILOT *(an hour later)*: We just lost another engine, so we'll be three hours late for our arrival.

PASSENGER: If the last engine dies, we'll be up here forever.


Why are airports always so far from town?
*Because they want them out where the planes are.*

Why do most ships sail the same routes?

*Pier pressure.*

When don't airline employees wear uniforms?

*When they're in plane clothes.*

Why don't dogs like to travel on planes?

*Because they suffer from jet wag.*

What squawks and jumps out of airplanes?

*A parrot-trooper.*

Why do pilots always fly past Peter Pan's island?

*Because the sign says "NEVER NEVER LAND."*

Knock-Knock.
> Who's there?

Yachts.
> Yachts who?

Yachts new, Pussycat?

What's the most unpleasant ship to travel on?
> *A hardship.*

Where do you find bargains at sea?
*On sale boats.*

What do you say when you want to stop a ship?
*"Whoa, whoa, whoa the boat...."*

What do ships eat for breakfast?
*Boatmeal.*

SHIP'S CAPTAIN: Quick, operator! Get me an SOS!
OPERATOR: Sure. How do you spell that?

# 23. TALK
# OF THE TOWN

Knock-Knock.

 Who's there?

Shutter.

 Shutter who?

Shutter up – she's talking too loud.

What animal talks too much?
*A yak.*

How do billboards talk?
*They use sign language.*

How do amoebas talk to each other?
*With cell phones.*

What cell phones do lizards use?
*Repdials.*

How do skunks call home?
*On smellular phones.*

How do pants address mail to each other?
*With zipper codes.*

How do buzzing insects talk to each other?

*They use bee-mail.*

How do baseball players keep in contact with their friends?

*They touch base with them.*

Why couldn't Tarzan call Jane?

*Her vine was busy.*

Why didn't the lamb make a sound all day?

*It didn't want to bleat between meals.*

What did the big hand on the clock say to the little hand?

*"I'll be back in an hour."*

# 24. EATING IT UP

Where does smart butter go?
*Honor roll.*

What do skeletons say before eating?
*"Bone appetit."*

What is an ape's favorite kind of cookie?
  *Chocolate chimp.*

What's a hamburger's favorite fairy tale?
  *"Hansel and Gristle."*

If you really like coffee, what train do you take?
  *An espresso.*

What trains carry bubble gum?
  *Chew chew trains.*

Where do you find silverware on a highway?
  *At the fork in the road.*

Knock-Knock.

Who's there?

Deena.

Deena who?

Deena is ready.

What do models eat off?

*Fashion plates.*

Why are frogs usually so happy?

*They get to eat what bugs them.*

SISTER: Mom wants you to come in and fix dinner.

BROTHER: Why? Is it broken?

What do geeks and nerds eat?

*Square meals.*

"I don't like the cheese with the holes in it."

"Then just eat the cheese and leave the holes on your plate."

"There's a mouse in the kitchen."

"Let it alone. Mice are supposed to be lucky."

"This one certainly is. It ate your lunch."

CUSTOMER: What dressing do you have for the salad?

WAITER: Blue cheese.

CUSTOMER: What other colors have you got?

What's good on bread but bad on the road?
*Jam.*

Why did the three hammers go to dinner?
*They were serving pound cake.*

Why did the cranberry turn red?
*It saw the turkey dressing.*

What do you call a cranberry that eats another cranberry?

*A crannibal.*

What are unhappy cranberries called?

*Blueberries.*

What do you call a banana that's been stepped on?

*A banana splat.*

How did the peach feel after it was eaten?

*Pit-iful.*

What side dish does a miner eat?

*Coal slaw.*

PEANUT: Would you go out with me?
CASHEW: Are you nuts?

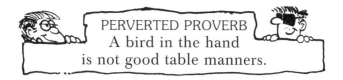

PERVERTED PROVERB
A bird in the hand
is not good table manners.

226

Did you hear what happened when they crossed an ostrich with a turkey to get bigger drumsticks? They got a scrawny bird that stuck its head in the mashed potatoes.

How can you give up cooking Thanksgiving dinner?
*Go cold turkey.*

What was the hardest part of preparing Thanksgiving dinner in prehistoric times?
*Stuffing the brontosaurus.*

MOTHER: Didn't I ask you to notice when the soup boiled over?
DAUGHTER: I did, Mom. It was at 7:30.

WARPED WISE MAN SAYS

Time flies like an arrow;
fruit flies like bananas.

Have you heard about the cannibal who loved fast food? He ordered a pizza with everyone on it.

... I LOVE TO SERVE MY FELLOW MAN!..

When does a chef know he's in trouble?
*When his goose is cooked.*

Why was the gossipy chef fired?
*Because he dished out the dirt.*

Why was the clumsy cook fired?
*She spilled the beans.*

What transportation do chefs prefer?
*The gravy train.*

"I've got my boyfriend to the point where he eats out of my hand."

"Saves a lot of dishwashing, doesn't it?"

"I've been cooking for years."

"Then I guess dinner must be ready now."

Where do mummies go for pizza?

*Pizza Tut.*

Why did the chef's spaghetti fall apart?
*He forgot the tomato paste.*

On what days do spiders have a good meal?

*On Flyday.*

What do spiders eat with their burgers?

*French flies.*

SPIDER: Will you share your curds with me?

MISS MUFFET: No whey.

What's the difference between mice and rice?

*You can't throw mice at weddings.*

Did you hear about the cannibal wedding party? They toasted the bride and groom.

Knock-Knock.

Who's there?

Queasy.

Queasy who?

Queasy as 1, 2, 3.

ARMY COOK: Don't waste food like that. You should eat it. You know the old saying, "Food will win the war."

SOLDIER: I believe that. But how are we going to get the enemy to eat it?

RANDY: I'll make dinner. Guests will be dropping over.

MANDY: They will if they eat your dinner.

"I finally trained my dog not to beg at the table."

"How did you do that?"

"I let him taste my cooking."

MANDY: The two things I cook best are apple dumplings and meat loaf.

SANDY: Which is this?

MOTHER: Did your boyfriend enjoy the dinner you made him last night?

DAUGHTER: I guess so. He said he hasn't been able to eat anything since.

What is Dracula's favorite dish?
*The quiche of death.*

When does Dracula find time to eat?
*During his coffin break.*

Duffy was baking a cake and suddenly ran away. Why did he do that?
*The recipe said, "Break an egg and beat it."*

CINDY: The recipe says that when the sauce starts to boil, you should add two teaspoons of water.

MINDY: Level or heaping?

What is a millionaire's favorite candy?
*Mints.*

What is a scientist's favorite candy?
*Experi-mints.*

"Did you finish first in the pie-eating contest?"

"No, I finished sickened."

What's red, white, and blue?

    *Sad candy canes.*

What do you call a croissant on roller skates?

    *Breakfast to go.*

Why did the poppy seed cross the road?
*It was on a roll.*

What makes a loaf of bread happy?
*Being kneaded.*

What do bread bakers do on their day off?
*Loaf.*

What do police officers buy at the bakery?
*Copcakes.*

How do you keep bagels from being stolen?
*Put lox on them.*

What did the gingerbread man find on his bed?
*A cookie sheet.*

"I'm the new manager of the doughnut shop."

"Are you in charge of everything?"

"Yes, the hole works."

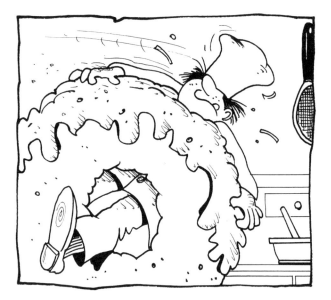

CUSTOMER: I want my money back! This
bread is full of holes.

BAKER: Of course it is. It's hole-wheat
bread.

What's green with red spots?
*A pickle with chicken pox.*

What's green, sour, and weighs over five tons?
*A picklesaurus.*

What do you call a pickle that draws?
*A dillustrator.*

What do you call a pickle that can add, subtract, multiply, and divide?
*A cuculator.*

Why did the cucumber hire a lawyer?
*Because it was in a pickle.*

Why did the cook try to make the cucumber laugh?

*To see if it was picklish.*


What would you get if you dropped your ice cream on the floor?

*A plopsicle.*


What would you get if you crossed chocolate pudding with your mother's high-heeled shoes?

*Yelled at!*

# 25. OH, HORRORS!

What monster is big and gray and wears a mask?

*The Elephant-om of the Opera.*

Knock-Knock.

   Who's there?

Derby.

   Derby who?

Derby ghosts in that haunted house.

What authors work on Halloween?
*Ghost writers.*

What's a ghost's favorite position?
*Horror-zontal.*

What do little ghosts prefer to frisbees?
*Boo-merangs.*

What's large and yellow and lives in Scotland?
*The Loch Ness canary.*

What kind of coffee does a vampire drink?
*De-coffinated.*

Why was the Invisible Man depressed?
*He was all dressed up with no face to go.*

What would you get if you crossed the Frankenstein monster with a pig?

*Frankenswine.*

What would you get if you crossed a monster with a heavy rainstorm?

A horrorcane.

What happened when the monster ate the electric company?

*It was in shock for a week.*

Why did the skeleton cross the road?

*To get to the body shop.*

Why can't skeletons play music in church?

*They have no organs.*

Why were the bones chasing the skull?
*They wanted to get ahead.*

Where do monsters buy their cookies?
*From the Ghoul Scouts.*

How does a witch tell time?

*With a witch watch.*

How many witches does it take to change a lightbulb?

*Only one, but it turns it into a toad.*

How do witches break the sound barrier?

*With a sonic broom.*

What packages does a witch carry on her broom?

*Hexpress mail.*

What do you get when you put a witch in the refrigerator?

*A cold spell.*

How do you make a witch itch?

*Take away her "W".*

What do you call two witches who live together?

*Broom mates.*

# 26. ON THE NET

What creature helps repair computers?
  *Debug.*

How do you praise a computer?
  *You say, "Data boy!"*

How did the computers afford a vacation?
  *They all chipped in.*

How does a computer eat?
  *A byte here and a byte there.*

What's a computer's favorite snack?
  *Micro-chips.*

What happened when they crossed a pit bull with a computer?
  *Its bark was worse than its megabyte.*

What did the baby computer say to its mother?
  *"I want my data."*

What did the lumberjack do with his computer?

*He logged on.*

What do you call brilliant Internet users?

*Star tekkies.*

What did the computer program and the itchy dog have in common?

*Bugs.*

What's a computer sign of old age?

*Loss of memory.*

What ailment do computers get most often?

*A slipped disk.*

Why did the computer hacker refuse to kill spiders?

*Because he needed the web sites.*

What did the mouse send over the Internet?

*Eeek-mail.*

Why did the computer stay home from school?

*It had a virus.*

What did the computer do in Hawaii?
 *Surf the Net.*

What's an astronaut's favorite spot on the computer keyboard?
 *The space bar.*

How did the computer do on its driving test?

*It crashed.*

What game did the computer play?

*Teck-tock-toe.*

Why wouldn't the cleaning lady operate the computer?

*She didn't do windows.*

# 27. LOVE AND KISSES

What kind of shoes did the plumber wear when he went dancing?

*Tap shoes.*

Where do Easter bunnies dance?

*At the basket ball.*

What did the girl centipede say to the boy centipede at the dance?

*"You're stepping on my foot, my foot, my foot. . ."*

How do dogs dance in Oz?
*On their tippy Totos.*

How do you make a strawberry swirl?
*Send it to ballet school.*

What dance do opticians attend?
*The eye ball.*

What's big, gray, floppy, and goes "Hoppity,
BOOM, hoppity, BOOM, hoppity,
BOOM"?
*The Easter Elephant.*

Do barbers like to dance?
*No, they just like to cut in.*

Why didn't the bicycle go dancing?
*It was two tired.*

What did the boy egg say to the girl egg?
*"Shell we dance?"*

What did the girl cow say to the boy cow?
*"Let's smooo-ch."*

Did you hear about the hair stylist who got rid of her boyfriend? She gave him the brush.

Where does a rabbit go when it needs grooming?
*To the hare dresser.*

What three ways do men wear their hair?

*Parted, unparted, and departed.*

What do you call a silly balloon?

*An airhead.*

Did you hear about the woman who put too much mousse on her hair? She grew antlers.

"I hear you broke off your engagement. What happened?

"Oh, it's just that my feeling for him has changed."

"Are you returning the ring?"

"Oh, no. My feeling for the ring hasn't changed."

Why did the fungi leave the party early?
*Because there wasn't mushroom.*

What is the longest line at a joker's party?
*The punch line.*

MAN: Doctor, is it okay to marry an octopus?

DOCTOR: Of course not.

MAN: One more thing. Do you know anybody who wants to buy eight engagement rings?

FROG *(telephoning the psychic line)*: Can you tell my future?

PSYCHIC: You are going to meet a beautiful woman who will be very curious about you.

FROG: That's great. Will I meet her at a party?

PSYCHIC: No, next semester in biology class.

What time do crocodiles meet their dates?

*Date o'croc.*

"Did you hear about the actress who fell off her seven-inch heels?"

"Was she hurt?"

"No, her eyelashes broke her fall."

Did the actress stop dating the movie star?

*Yes, he's out of the picture.*

Knock-Knock.

Who's there?

Amarillo.

Amarillo who?

Amarillo-fashioned girl.

SHE: Am I the first girl you ever kissed?

He: Now that you mention it, your face is familiar.

What do you call a ghost and a zombie that go out on a date?

*Boo-friend and ghoul-friend.*

YOUNG MAN: Miss, would you go out with me tonight?

YOUNG WOMAN: I don't go out with perfect strangers.

YOUNG MAN: I never said I was perfect.

"I was out with a nurse last night."

"Well, if you behave yourself, maybe they'll let you out without one."

What happened when the boy snake and the girl snake got into an argument?

*They hissed and made up.*

"Look at the beautiful bunch of roses I got for my girlfriend."

"Wow, how did you swing a trade like that?"

What do you call two recently married dandelions?

*Newlyweeds.*

Why did the cow want a divorce?

*Because she had a bum steer.*

LITTLE ASHLEY:  When I get older, I'm going to marry the boy next door.

VISITOR: Why is that?

LITTLE ASHLEY:  Cause I'm not allowed to cross the street.

When two bullets get married what do they have?

*BB's.*

Why doesn't the melon get married?

*Because it cantaloupe.*

What did Benjamin Franklin's wife tell him?

*To go fly a kite.*

What would you call a girl with four boyfriends named William?

*A Bill collector.*

BOY: Well, I'll see you pretty soon.
GIRL: Oh? You don't think I'm pretty now?

What do you call it when spiders marry?

*A webbing.*

How do poets take their wedding vows?

*For better or verse.*

When do bedbugs get married?

*In the spring.*

# 28. ARTS AND ENTERTAINMENT

Knock-Knock.

> Who's there?

Alistair.

> Alistair who?

Alistair at the TV until I fall asleep.

What does a funny train ride on?

*A laugh track.*

FRED: Don't you wish life were like television?

NED: I can't answer that now.

FRED: Why not?

NED: I'm on a commercial break.

TV REPAIRMAN: What seems to be the trouble with your TV, ma'am?

WOMAN: It seems to have double images. I hope you men can fix it.

Is it possible to lose your television clicker?

*It's a remote possibility.*

What TV channel do horses watch?

*Hay B.C.*

Why don't fish watch TV?

*They don't want to get hooked on it.*

How did the gymnast watch television?

*She flipped through the channels.*

Why did the talk show hostess discuss forest fires?

*It was a hot topic.*

Why did the comedian quit his job?

*He was at his wit's end.*

How did the puppet get into show business?

*His friends pulled a few strings for him.*

Why are set designers difficult?

*They make scenes.*

MAGICIAN: I do one of the greatest tricks of all time. I saw a woman in half.

AGENT: You call that a great trick! Magicians have been doing that for years.

MAGICIAN: Really? Lengthwise?

What would you get if you crossed a magician with a photographer?

*A lot of hocus focus.*

Knock-Knock.
   Who's there?
Abner.
   Abner who?
Abner-cadabra!

"I saw a really bad magician last week."

"What was his best trick?"

"He made the audience disappear."

DIRECTOR: Now in this scene you jump off the cliff.

ACTOR: But suppose I get killed?

DIRECTOR: Don't worry – it's the last scene in the film.

AGENT *(to writer)*: I've got good news and bad news.

WRITER: What's the good news?

AGENT: Paramount loved your story, absolutely ate it up.

WRITER: What's the bad news?

AGENT: Paramount is my cocker spaniel.

Why couldn't the writer cross the road?
   *He had authoritis.*

Can the king's son write longhand?
   *No, but he prince.*

What are a writer's least favorite toys?

*Writer's blocks.*

Why did the king think that he could write a book?

*He already had a title.*


If a skunk wrote a book, what list would it be on?

*The best smeller list.*

## BOOKS NEVER WRITTEN

*Is Your Family Well?* by Howard D. Folks.

*The Broken Window Mystery* by Eva Brick.

*Cattle Ranching* by Brandon D. Bull.

*Bullfighting Mistakes* by Gordon Bluddy.

*Choosing a Pet Bird* by Perry Keat.

Why did it take the monster two months to finish the book?

*It wasn't hungry.*


Where do books sleep?

*Under their covers.*


What do you call a script for a horror movie?

*A screamplay.*


Why did the writer work in the basement?

*He wanted to write a best cellar.*


POET: Do you think I should put more fire in my poetry?

PUBLISHER: No, I think you should put more poetry in the fire.

"Scientists believe that cavemen made the first music by banging stones together."

"Gee, I guess that was the first rock music."

A woman walked into a music store and asked about a used piano. "This one here must be very old. The keys are all yellow."

"No, the piano isn't old," said the salesman. "It's just that the elephant was a heavy smoker."

What do you call a flutist after he's eaten a lot of candy?

*A hyper viper.*

"My brother has been playing the guitar for ten years now."

"He must be pretty good."

"Not really. It took him nine years to find out that he wasn't supposed to blow through it."

Why do bagpipers walk so fast when they play?

*To get away from the noise.*

"My upstairs neighbors are so loud. Yesterday they kept banging on the floor all night."

"Did they wake you?"

"No, fortunately I was playing my tuba."

What comes after a tuba?

*A three-ba.*

Why do elephants trumpet?

*They don't know how to play the violin.*

What would you get if you crossed a slob with an artist?

*A messterpiece.*

What's green and smells like paint?
*Paint.*

Who lives underground and loves to paint?
*Vincent Van Gopher.*

Why did the sculptor think he was going crazy?
*He lost his marbles.*

What happened when the artist threw a tantrum?
*He showed his true colors.*

Did you hear about the graffiti artist who retired?  He saw the handwriting on the wall.

What are the chances of an artist making a living?

*They're sketchy.*

How do artists become famous?

*It's the luck of the draw.*

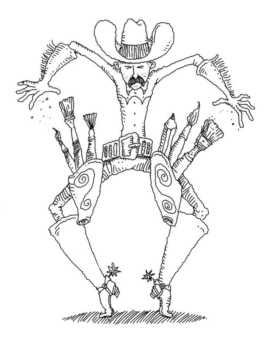

What is the most famous skunk statue in Egypt?

*The Stinx.*

How do you carve a statue out of wood?

*Whittle by whittle.*

# 29. EATING OUT!

What do monsters order in fast-food restaurants?

*French frights.*

"This restaurant has great food. I ordered a fresh egg and got the freshest egg in the world. I ordered a cup of hot coffee and got the hottest coffee in the world."

"Yes, I know. I ordered a small steak."

A man walked into a restaurant that boasted it could supply any dish that the customer ordered.

"I'll have an elephant sandwich with ketchup," he said.

The waiter returned a few minutes later empty-handed. "I'm sorry, sir," he said, "but we've run out of ketchup."

CUSTOMER: Waiter, there's a fly in my soup!

WAITER: Wait a minute, I'll get you a fork.

CUSTOMER: Waiter, there's a fly in my
  soup.
WAITER: Sorry, sir, did you order without?

CUSTOMER: Do you serve crabs here?
WAITER: We serve everybody. Have a seat.

CUSTOMER: Waiter, there's a twig in my soup.

WAITER: That's no surprise, we have branches everywhere.

CUSTOMER: Miss, you have your finger in my soup.

WAITRESS: That's all right, it's not hot.

"How was that new restaurant you ate in?"

"Terrible! It's so bad they can't give out doggy bags because it would be cruelty to animals."

DINER #1: I've heard that scientists say we are what we eat.
DINER #2: Oh, let's order something rich!

"Why did you give that hat check girl a $5 tip?"

"Look at the great-looking hat she gave me!"

"Why are you upset?"

"I saw a sign in the restaurant that said 'Watch your coat and hat,' so I did and someone stole my dinner."

Why are fast-food restaurants so
dangerous?

*You might bump into a man eating chicken.*

"Waiter, look at this chicken you served me. One leg is shorter than the other."

"Were you planning to eat it or to dance with it?"

CUSTOMER: What's that fly doing in my alphabet soup?

WAITER: Trying to learn to read.

CUSTOMER: What's that fly doing in my ice cream?

WAITER: Probably cooling off. It gets pretty hot in the kitchen.

CUSTOMER: Waiter, there's a fly in my soup!

WAITER: Quick! Throw him some water wings!

CUSTOMER: Give me something to eat and
   make it snappy.
WAITER: How about a crocodile sandwich?

WAITER: You ought to give me a tip. Why, every champion cheapskate that comes into this place gives me at least a quarter.

CUSTOMER: Meet the new champ.

MAN: I'd like a glass of ginger ale.

WAITER: Pale?

MAN: No, a glass will be enough.

CUSTOMER: I'd like a cup of coffee.

FRIEND: I'd like one too, and make sure it's in a clean cup.

WAITRESS *(bringing back the coffee)*: Okay, which one ordered the clean cup?

"Waiter, this menu is blank on one side."
    "That's in case you're not hungry."

MAGICIAN (*in a restaurant*): That rabbit stew you served me tasted horrible. I'll never come here again.

WAITER: Well, that's the first time a rabbit made a magician disappear!

"Boy, this food is really terrible," said the diner.

"Gee," said the waiter. "Anything else wrong?

"Yeah," said the customer, "the portions are too small."

DINER: I'll have what the man at the next table is having.

WAITER: Okay, but I don't think he'll be too happy about it.

CUSTOMER: Look at this chicken. It's
nothing but skin and bones.

WAITER: Yes, sir. Would you like the
feathers, too?

WAITER: I recommend the fish. It's been our specialty for years.

CUSTOMER: Well, bring me something you haven't had for so long.

What type of writing does a waiter use? *Menu-script.*

CUSTOMER: This steak you brought me is rare. I said "well done."

WAITRESS: Thank you sir, I don't get many compliments.

CUSTOMER: You call this beef noodle soup your special? I can't find any beef or noodles in it.

WAITER: That's what makes it so special.

What did the teddy bear say after dining out?

"I'm stuffed."

Where does a turtle go to eat out?

A slow-food restaurant.

# 30. SPORT AND GAMES

Why don't rabbits play football?

*Their ears don't fit in the helmet.*

What do you call a person who does arithmetic and scores touchdowns?

*A mathlete.*


Where do athletes like to stay?

*In shape.*


What weights do beginning bodybuilders use?

*Paperweights.*


What animal lives in a gym?

*A gympanzee.*


How did the busy track star do his homework?

*On the run.*

What farm animal is the best boxer?
  *Duck.*

Why couldn't the boxer start a fire?
  *Because he lost all his matches.*

"I asked my mother for a new pair of sneakers for gym."

"What did she say?"

"She said to tell Jim to buy his own sneakers."

"My brother is so dumb."

"How dumb is he?"

"He got a pair of water skis for his birthday. Now he's looking for a lake with a hill in it."

"You shouldn't swim on a full stomach."

"Okay, I'll swim on my back."

What furniture is designed for those who like swimming outdoors?

*A birdbath.*

Knock-Knock.

 Who's there?

Wiener.

 Wiener who?

Wiener and still champion!

What class does soda pop go to?

*Fizz ed.*

Was the turtle and rabbit race close?

*Yes, it was won by a hare.*

What happened when the silkworms had a race?

*It ended in a tie.*

How did the karate student feel about failing the test?

*He could kick himself.*

What illness can you catch from a martial arts expert?

*Kung flu.*

Knock-Knock.
  Who's there?
Aikido.
  Aikido who?
Aikido you not.

SOCCER PLAYER: Did you see how close I
  came to making that goal? I could
  kick myself for missing it.
COACH: Don't bother. You'd probably miss.

What position does a monster play on a soccer team?

*Ghoulie.*

What did the basketball player ask for from his fairy godmother?

*Three swishes.*

What did the basketball player do at breakfast?

*Dunk donuts.*

Why did the retired basketball player become a judge?

*So he could stay on the court.*

WARPED
WISE MAN SAYS:

Basketball is
a lot of hoopla.

How do they play basketball in Hawaii?
*With a hula hoop.*

What do frogs do when they play basketball?

*They take jump shots.*

What is the difference between a basketball player and a tired dog?

*The ballplayer wears a uniform, the dog only pants.*

What kind of uniform do women basketball players wear?

*Hoop skirts.*

What do mice wear to play basketball?

*Squeakers.*

What is a psychic's favorite sport?

*Crystal ball.*

Why are the floors of basketball courts wet?

*The players dribble a lot.*

Why did the basketball player hold his nose?

*Someone was taking a foul shot.*

When shouldn't a mountain climber yell for help?

*When he's hanging by his teeth.*

How did the mountain climber feel when he tumbled off the cliff?

*Crestfallen.*

Why did the aging climber refuse to scale the mountain?

*He was already over the hill.*

The reason mountain climbers rope themselves together is to prevent the smart ones from going home.

Why did the golf ball get mad at the golf club?

*It was teed off.*

What did the hole say to the golf ball?

*"Why don't you drop in sometime?"*

What's yellow and goes "putt, putt, putt"?
*A canary playing golf.*

GOLFER: Notice the improvement since last year?
CADDY: Yes, you had your clubs shined, didn't you?

GOLFER: Caddy, how would you have played that last shot?
CADDY: Under an assumed name.

"Playing golf can be bad for your health."

"What makes you say that?"

"I just heard a golfer saying he had four strokes on the first hole."

GOLFER *(on golf course)*: Before I hire you, caddy, tell me, are you good at finding lost golf balls?

CADDY: Yes, sir, I'm the best.

GOLFER: Great! You're hired. Now go out and find us some golf balls so we can start the game.

How did the golfer waste time?

*Puttering around.*

Golf is no longer a rich man's sport. There are millions of poor players.

"My uncle once tracked a deer in his pajamas."

"How did the deer get into your uncle's pajamas?"

GAME WARDEN: Didn't you see the sign —
"NO FISHING ALLOWED"?

KID: That's okay. I'm fishing silently.

GAME WARDEN: Young man, there is no fishing here.

BOY: I'm not fishing. I'm washing my pet worm.

Two fishermen, Lem and Clem, made a bet on who could catch the first fish. Lem got a bite and was so excited that he fell off the pier.

"Hey," said Clem, "if you're going to dive for them, the bet is off."

Bud and Bubba rented a boat and fished a lake for several hours. They caught over 20 fish. Bud said to Bubba, "Mark this spot so we can come back to it tomorrow."

The next day, when they were gong to rent the boat, Bud said, "Did you mark the spot?"

"Yeah," said Bubba. "I put a big X on the side of the boat."

"You fool!" said Bud. "What if we don't get the same boat?"

# 31. SEASON'S GREETINGS

Where does Santa go swimming?
*At the North Pool.*

Knock-Knock.

Who's there?

Aloha.

Aloha who?

Aloha myself down the chimney.

What do clams and oysters do over the holidays?

*Shellebrate.*

What did the big grape say to the little grape on Christmas?

*"'Tis the season to be jelly."*

What does a Christmas tree eat with?

*Utinsels.*

Why did the turkey cross the road?

*The chicken retired and moved to Florida.*

What did St. Nicholas build when he wanted a place to put his clothes?

*A Santa Closet.*

What's Tarzan's favorite Christmas song?
*"Jungle Bells."*

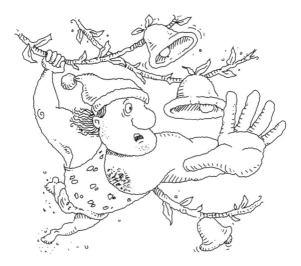

Why was Rudolph wet?
*Because of the rain, dear.*

Who was Scrooge?

*The Wizard of Bahs.*

What does Scrooge wear to play ice hockey?

*Cheap skates.*

What kind of mail did Scrooge get from Marley?

*Chain letters.*

What kind of paste do they use at the North Pole?

*Igloo.*

What do you get from a vampire at the North Pole?

*Frost bite.*

What's a frog's favorite thing at Christmas?
*Mistletoad.*

# 32. DOING BUSINESS

"I heard about a man who invented a hair tonic that can grow hair on a bowling ball."

"Did he make a lot of money?"

"No. Nobody wanted hairy bowling balls."

DING: I opened a new business. I started
making lamps out of vegetables.

DONG: What are they for?

DING: People on a light diet.

MASKED MAN: Do you have flowers for all occasions?

FLORIST: Yes, we do. What's the occasion?

MASKED MAN: This is a stickup.


LADY *(at florist)*: I want a dozen roses for my daughter's coming-out party.

FLORIST: It's none of my business, but what was she put away for?


What do you call a flower shop that's burning down?

*A florist fire.*


BOSS: Did you mark the crate "FRAGILE, THIS SIDE UP," the way I told you?

WORKER: Yes, sir, and just to be safe, I marked it that way on both sides.

"I'm sorry to hear that your factory burned down. What did you manufacture?"

"Fire extinguishers."

CUSTOMER: I'd like to buy a piano. Does it come with a guarantee?

SALESMAN: Yes, we guarantee it's a piano.

MANAGER: You're 30 minutes late. Don't you know what time we start here?

OFFICE BOY: No, by the time I get here, everyone is already working.

BOSS: You're certainly asking for a big salary for a man with no experience.

JOB APPLICANT: Yes, but it's much harder work when you don't know what you're doing.

BOSS: Before I hire you, I have to ask, do you have a previous record?

JOB APPLICANT: No, I've never been caught.

# 33. DOCTOR, DOCTOR

Why does a turtle live in a shell?

*Because it can't afford an apartment.*

Why did the cookie go to the doctor?
   *It was feeling crumby.*

"Does your doctor make house calls?"
   "Yes, but your house has to be very
sick."

Why did the fisherman go to the doctor?
*He lost his herring.*

Why did the bee go to the doctor?
*It had hives.*

Why did the old house go to the doctor?
*It was having windowpanes.*

What illness is caused by the third letter of the alphabet?
*C-sickness.*

SURGEON: I have to bring this suit back. It's all wrong.

TAILOR: What's wrong with it?

SURGEON: I don't know. It was all right until I took out the stitches.

336

PATIENT: Doctor, I keep seeing spots.
DOCTOR: Have you seen a psychiatrist?
PATIENT: No, just spots.

Why did the banana go to the doctor?
*It wasn't peeling well.*

PSYCHIATRIST: Why do you now say you are George Washington? On your last visit here you said you were Napoleon Bonaparte.

PATIENT: Yes, but that was by my first mother.

PATIENT: I'm always dizzy for half an hour after I get up in the morning.

DOCTOR: Well, try getting up half an hour later.

PATIENT: Doc, you've got to help me. I snore so loudly that I wake myself up.

DOCTOR: In that case, sleep in another room.

How do you measure poison ivy?

*By itches.*

**338**

DOCTOR: You really need glasses.
PATIENT: I'm already wearing glasses.
DOCTOR: In that case, I need glasses.


PATIENT: Doctor, I'm feeling a bit
    schizophrenic.
DOCTOR: That makes four of us.


"Doctor, I was playing the flute when I suddenly swallowed it."

"Well, let's look on the bright side. You could have been playing the piano."


"My doctor is slow."

"How slow is he?"

"He's so slow, he doesn't have magazines in his waiting room – he has novels."

How did the sick lamb get to the hospital?

*By lambulance.*

# 34. HOME SWEET HOME

Knock-Knock.

Who's there?

Thermos.

Thermos who?

Thermos be a doorbell around here somewhere.

What do you get when you squeeze a curtain?

*Drape juice.*

Did you hear about the lawn mower? It got tired of being pushed around.

Why is a leaky faucet like a racehorse?

*Because it's off and running.*

What would you get if you crossed a cold with a leaky faucet?

*Cough drops.*

What happens when you don't dust your mirror?

*You get a dirty look.*

Why did the fireplace call the doctor?
*Because its chimney had the flu.*

Why is coal one of the best fuels ever used?
*Because there is no fuel like an old fuel.*

What did they use to clean the *Starship Enterprise*?

  *Spock 'n' Span.*

What happened to the guy who got his head stuck in the washing machine?

*He got brainwashed.*

What did one clothesline say to the other clothesline?

*"You don't have any clothes on."*

What happened when the broom competed against the dustpan?

*It was a clean sweep.*

CUSTOMER: Could I put this wallpaper on myself?

CLERK: I guess so, but it would look better on the wall.

"May I speak with the general?"

"I'm sorry, but the general is out sick today."

"What made him sick?"

"Oh, things in general."

# INDEX

**348**

**349**

**350**

**351**

# If you liked this book, you'll love all the titles in this series: